Table of Contents

The Organisation and Operation of Community Mental Health Teams in England

A National Survey

by Steve Onyett, Tracey Heppleston and Diane Bushnell

ISBN   1 870480 11 2

Published by
The Sainsbury Centre for Mental Health
134 – 138 Borough High Street
London
SE1 1LB

071 403 8790

Acknowledgements

This research was supported by a grant from The Gatsby Charitable Foundation. We would like to thank Kim Hitchcock for conducting the telephone survey and assisting with the early stages of the research, and Vida Field, Geoff Shepherd and Matt Muijen for sharing their knowledge and experience with us. Maureen McManus prepared the final report and Patricia Louis and Karen Lorimer provided dedicated administrative support.

Introduction

Recent guidance on the care programme approach and care management has again underlined the importance of multidisciplinary team working for people with severe and long-term mental health problems (DoH, 1990; DoH/SSI, 1991). Multidisciplinary team working is central to the provision of comprehensive, coordinated and continuous community care (Shepherd, 1994) and the principal vehicle of this work is likely to remain community mental health teams (CMHTs), often based in buildings referred to as community mental health centres (CMHCs).

There are strong parallels between the UK and American experiences of CMHTs. Here, CMHTs have been criticised for neglect of people with severe and long-term mental health problems (Sayce, Craig and Boardman, 1991; Patmore and Weaver, 1992) as were the American CMHCs established subsequent to the 1963 Community Mental Health Centres Act (Dowell and Ciarlo, 1983). This legislation created a greater diversity of service provision in the USA but also meant that people with continuing health and social care needs had to navigate a fragmented and uncoordinated provider system. The American response was to establish "community support systems" with greater emphasis on case management to coordinate an appropriate range of relevant services. From the mid-1970s to the present, therefore, evaluation of American CMHTs has thus become broadly synonymous with evaluations of case management (Onyett, 1992).

Similar concerns about the fragmentation and distortion of mental health service planning and provision has recently been raised in the UK (Mental Health Act Commission, 1993; Morris and Davidson, 1992) and case (or latterly care) management has been invoked to make the most effective use of available resources (Ford, Cooke and Repper, 1992; Onyett, 1992). As in America, approaches relying on more assertive methods of providing care have been found to achieve good results in clinical and social outcome, user satisfaction, service use and cost (e.g. Burns *et al.*, 1993; Merson *et al.*, 1992; Muijen *et al.*, 1992).

Despite the acknowledged importance of multidisciplinary teams, and recognition of their potential strengths and weaknesses, theoretical formulations of effective team working have been scarce. Ovretveit provides the only attempt to delineate models of multidisciplinary mental health team management and organisation (Ovretveit, 1993). He describes teams along three dimensions: structure, process and integration. Structure refers to the composition of the team and how it is managed. Process describes how referrals are received by the team and how the team works with service users over time. Integration refers to the "closeness" of working between members. He contrasts "network-association teams" with "formal teams". Practitioners within networks come together on a voluntary basis, each managed by their own professional line management. Formal teams require a team leader and collective responsibility for specified objectives. They are further subdivided according to the balance of core full-time to part-time staff and the team leader's responsibilities for their work.

Ovretveit described the design of team process as a series of logical stages: (1) deciding on acceptable referral sources; publicising the service accordingly and providing optimal means of access; (2) receiving referrals in a way that allows the effective planning of assessment or an emergency response where necessary; (3) determining criteria for acceptance for assessment; (4) allocating referrals for assessment; (5) assessment; (6) acceptance for longer term work; (7) allocation for longer term work; (8) intervention and/or monitoring; (9) team review; and (10) closure. The design of this process should aim to achieve the optimal match between the team member's collective resources of knowledge, skills, experience and time, and the needs of their identified client group. Informed decisions are required about the priority and resources allocated to each stage.

Ovretveit's categories have provided a useful framework for service development but whether they actually reflect the configuration of existing teams has not been investigated. Indeed, there remains a paucity of research on the organisation and operation of CMHTs aside from single service evaluations (e.g. McAusland, 1985) and studies of Government demonstration projects (e.g. Patmore and Weaver, 1991; Knapp et al., 1992). The problems of generalisation from demonstration projects are well known (Bachrach, 1980) and underline the need to investigate services with more ordinary histories.

This report has three main aims:

1. To describe the organisation and operation of CMHTs in England;

2. To examine those features associated with teams reporting an emphasis on work with people with severe and long-term mental health problems;

3. To highlight associations among the organisational and operational features examined.

We hope that this report will provide useful guidance and a source of comparative data for individuals and authorities developing CMHTs at the present time.

Methodology

For a team to fulfil criteria for the study it had to: (1) be recognised by service managers as a multidisciplinary team comprising two or more disciplines; (2) serve adults with mental health problem as its identified client group; (3) do most of its work outside hospitals (although it may be hospital based); (4) have four or more members; and (5) offer a wider range of services than simply structured day care. Teams that were wholly dedicated to people over 75, people with drink or drug problems, or people with learning difficulties were excluded. This definition was adapted from a earlier survey conducted by The Sainsbury Centre for Mental Health in 1987–8 (Sayce, Craig and Boardman, 1991). This survey only examined CMHTs working in CMHCs where direct client work was carried out. The more permissive definition used in the present study aims to accommodate other models of care in the belief that this more authentically represents the current state of multidisciplinary community mental health team working in England. In practice, a team was defined as a CMHT because external managers defined it as such, even though it might otherwise fulfil none of the more usual requirements of research on work groups (e.g. Shea and Guzzo, 1987). Despite these differences, the 1987–8 survey provides the only comprehensive data available and will be used for qualified comparisons throughout this report.

Data was collected through a postal survey following a telephone survey. The aim of the telephone survey was to identify contact persons for specific teams who would either complete or organise the completion of a questionnaire on the organisation and operation of the team. It was anticipated that this would improve return rates by ensuring that the most appropriate individual had been identified and by providing an opportunity to personally explain the study and its aims. The telephone survey took place over the latter half of 1992 and the subsequent postal survey took place from the middle of January to the beginning of March 1993. The variables examined in the questionnaire are shown in Table 1.

Table 1 – Variables Examined in the Postal Survey

General Team Characteristics

Funding and managing authorities
Details of catchment area
Case-load mix
Numbers of staff joining or leaving team

Team Structure

Team composition
Team size
The sharing of a team base and its location
Service user and community member involvement
Extent of shared leadership within team
Allocation of management responsibilities

Team Process

Whether first contact point for locality
Accepted sources of referral
Method for receipt of referral
Pooling of referral before assessment
Frequency of clinical review meetings
Integration of record keeping
Team activity
Method for accessing hospital beds
Transfer of responsibilities following admission
Case/care management and keyworking roles

In order to improve the readability of this report information on statistical analysis is given in the Appendix and test statistics and significance levels are omitted. All associations reported are significant at the one percent level.

Results

Respondents

The Health Services Yearbook and previous contacts established by The Sainsbury Centre for Mental Health were used as first steps in making telephone contact with Districts. Respondents were asked to supply details of any teams known to them, including those managed by other agencies. Of 183 Districts in England, a conclusive contact was achieved for 175 (95.6%). The telephone survey identified 144 districts with teams relevant to the study, containing 290 contact persons reporting on 517 CMHTs. By the final deadline 329 questionnaires were returned, 26 of which were defined by the respondent as not appropriate according to our supplied criteria. One further team was excluded as apparently a large and uni-disciplinary service. The overall response rate was therefore 63.6% with 58.4% of the total identified population finally entered for analysis. Data from 109 Districts were collected (representing 75% of those with CMHTs and 60% of the total number of Districts).

Respondents were coded *post hoc* on the basis of their title. As can be seen from Table 2, team "leaders", "coordinators" and "managers" between them made up the largest group (35.4%).

Table 2 – Contact Persons Coded by Job Title

Respondents	N	%
Team "managers"	39	12.9
Team "coordinators"	46	15.2
Team "leaders"	22	7.3
Consultant psychiatrists	19	6.3
General managers	59	19.5
Senior nurse managers	17	5.6
CPN managers	8	2.6
Others	52	17.2
Missing	40	13.2

General CMHT Characteristics

Funding and managing authorities

The authorities funding and managing teams are shown in Table 3. Most teams were jointly funded by health and social services. Written comments on the form indicated that joint funding often involved social services full or part funding social work posts. Health authorities or trusts were the only sole agency funders. This may have reflected the study's multidisciplinary criteria for inclusion as a team or bias arising from deriving our sample through health contacts. The "other" category included a team joint funded by the Department of Health and a charity, and a team funded by a Trust who were paid by Local Authorities when their residents attended.

Table 3 – Agencies Funding and Managing CMHTs

Agency arrangement	Funding		Managing	
	N	%	N	%
Health authority/Trust only	108	35.8	142	47.0
Social services only	0	0	0	0
Voluntary, private or not-for profit organisation only	0	0	0	0
Health and social services	179	59.3	148	49.0
Health, social services and others	11	3.6	8	2.6
Other arrangement	4	1.3	4	1.3

Teams were evenly divided between those that were jointly managed by health and social services and those that were solely managed by a health authority or Trust. No teams were solely managed by social services or voluntary, private or not-for profit organisations. The four teams reporting other arrangements included a team that was directly managed by a Trust but was also overseen by a joint planning group, and one where members were employed by social services but managed by a Trust. Some DHAs or Trusts appear to be the sole managers of jointly funded teams. These include CMHTs where joint funding entails funding social work posts.

In the 1987–8 survey 69% of CMHCs were solely managed by District Health Authorities compared with only 41% in the present study. This appears to reflect a positive trend towards joint management.

Case-load mix

Severe mental health problems were defined as a level of distress or disturbance that could normally result in a diagnosis of psychosis, psychiatric admission, or community-based interventions to prevent admission. Long-term was indicated by intense service use (e.g. hospital admissions or weekly home visits) over six months or more. People suffering from organic illness, brain injury or extreme personal trauma were included. Estimates of the percentage of the team's caseload comprising people with severe and long-term mental health problems correlated with practitioner estimates of the percentage in their own caseloads in a random sample of 57 teams conducted four months subsequently (r = 0.46).

People with severe and long-term mental health problems comprised on average 57.1% of the teams caseload (median = 55%, SD = 24.5%). The distribution was not normal and was, therefore, divided up into four categories for much of the subsequent analysis. 32 teams (10.5%) reported a 100% dedication of caseload to this client group, 70 (23%) between 66% and 99%, 123 (40.5%) between 33% and 66% and 63 (20.7%) had less than 33%.

As the definition of severe and long-term mental health problems used in the study was derived and piloted specifically for a postal survey, direct comparisons with other studies are difficult. Patmore and Weaver (1991) found that 46% of their CMHTs caseloads comprised people with severe and long-term mental health problems using a similar definition.

Characteristics of the catchment area

The median size of catchment was 48 square miles with a median population of 60,000. Eleven (3.7%) teams did not have catchment areas.

Respondents were asked to classify the area that the team worked in as urban, rural or mixed using categories based on a study by Perlman, Hartman and Bosak, (1984). "Urban" was defined as within a city of town with a population of 50,000 or more, "rural" as an area where there was no town of 10,000 or more and where less than half the population lived in towns or villages of 2,500 or more, and "Mixed/suburban" as neither of the above. 130 teams (43%) operated in urban areas, 132 (44.1%) in mixed/suburban areas, and 37 (12.4%) in rural areas.

Urban teams had a significantly higher proportion of people with severe and long-term mental health problems (63%) than both rural (47%) and mixed or suburban teams (53.4%).

Staff turnover

The mean number of people joining teams over the previous year was 3.1 (median = 2, SD = 3.62) while the mean number of people leaving was 1.62, (median = 1, SD = 1.74). Taking the ratio of people joining to leaving per team as an index of growth, it did appear that the size of teams was increasing overall (mean = 1.87, SD = 2.7). This perhaps reflects the comparative youth of the teams sampled. Teams had been taking referrals for a mean of 3.93 years (median = 3, SD = 3.18, minimum = one month, maximum = 20 years).

Significantly more people joined and left urban teams in the previous year when compared with rural teams (mean = 3.7 versus 2.0 joining; 1.9 versus 1.0 leaving).

Team Structure

Team size

The mean size of teams was 11.4 (SD = 6.3, median = 9.6, minimum = 1.8, maximum = 48.5) in full-time equivalents (FTEs) and 15 (SD = 7.4, median = 13.0, minimum = 4, maximum = 52) in people. Teams with over 25 members were contacted by telephone and all fulfilled the study's eligibility criteria.

Team composition

Table 4 shows the percentage of teams containing each discipline. CPNs, social workers and administrative staff were the most frequently occurring disciplines in CMHTs. Consultant psychiatrists were the next most frequently occurring although as many as one fifth of CMHTs did not report having them as members. Although team managers, coordinators or leaders predominate a wide variety of personnel involved in the work of CMHTs was apparent among the personnel reported as "other".

Table 4 – Statistics on Team Composition

Discipline	% of teams containing discipline	Mean input per team FTEs (people)	Standard deviations FTEs (people)	Mean ratio of FTEs to people in teams	Ratio of frozen or unfilled posts to total FTE (count of FTE)
Community psychiatric nurses	93.4	3.55 (3.83)	2.60 (2.75)	.94	.04 (41.4)
Social workers	86.1	1.53 (1.87)	1.60 (1.92)	.85	.08 (34.3)
Administrative staff (including receptionists)	85.4	1.32 (1.87)	1.07 (1.57)	.75	.05 (17.9)
Nurses (other than CPNs)	33.8	1.01 (1.22)	3.10 (3.33)	.90	.06 (16.0)
Occupational therapists	68.9	0.75 (0.95)	0.76 (0.87)	.80	.21 (44.6)
Generic/support workers	37.7	0.65 (0.88)	1.58 (1.77)	.82	.11 (20.6)
Consultant psychiatrists	79.1	0.62 (1.02)	0.58 (0.78)	.64	.07 (8.10)
Doctors (other than consultants)	67.5	0.59 (1.34)	0.73 (1.18)	.57	.04 (6.70)
Clinical psychologists	71.5	0.50 (0.90)	0.52 (0.78)	.59	.30 (41.7)
Others	27.8	0.36 (0.57)	0.98 (1.24)	.73	.06 (6.20)
Other specialist therapists	31.8	0.21 (0.44)	0.52 (0.04)	.55	.06 (3.90)
Volunteer staff	13.9	0.07 (0.45)	0.38 (1.77)	.30	(None)

Table 4 also shows the mean number of people and full-time equivalents (FTEs) per team for each discipline. Disciplines are listed in descending order of FTEs per team. FTEs are emphasised in this analysis as this most accurately represents the human resources actually contributing to the work of the team.

The FTE input of each discipline was almost identical to that reported in the 1987–8 survey with the exception of increased input from generic/support workers (from 0.2 FTE) and decreased input from consultant psychiatrists (from 1.2 FTE). The standard deviations in Table 4 give an indication of the variation of scores. The typical pattern of distribution of FTE input for disciplines with large standard deviations in comparison with the mean indicated that a majority of teams had small FTE contributions with a few outlying teams receiving a large contribution. For example, 80% of teams had less that one FTE non-CPN nurse while 1% had more than 17. Similarly, while there were generally very few teams with generic/support workers, one had 17.4. For doctors other than consultants, 85% of teams had less than one while one team had 3.6.

Table 4 also shows the ratio of FTEs to people within teams. This provides an indicator of the extent of part-time working among each discipline (full-time equals one). Consultant psychiatrists, clinical psychologists and non-consultant doctors offered only part-time input (mean 0.64, 0.59 and 0.56 FTE per team respectively) and thus rank lower in their FTE contribution to teams when compared with their contribution measured in people. In contrast, generic/support workers, although few in number, tended to offer a more full-time commitment (mean = 0.82). Both groups of nurses offered the most full-time commitment with volunteer staff the least.

No significant associations between the FTE input to the team from the various disciplines and the proportion of people on the team's caseload with severe and long-term mental health problems were found. However, a strong association with the amount of part-time working (measured as the ratio of FTE to people per team) emerged. Teams with 100% of their caseload dedicated to people with severe and long-term mental health problems had significantly less part-time working that those with less than 66%.

Clinical psychologists and occupational therapists had a disproportionately high number of frozen or unfilled posts (see Table 4). Across disciplines the mean number of frozen or unfilled posts per team was 0.8.

The sharing of a team base

Most of the teams (90.4%) had a base shared by more than one discipline. A mean of 75% of the total number of people in the team shared the base (median = 0.77%, SD = 0.24%).

The team bases are shown in Table 5. The "residential"-based teams were either located in ordinary houses or institutional residential care settings. The "other" locations referred to a mixture of office accommodation, some shared with other agencies. Although CMHCs dominated, a large proportion of teams remained attached to hospital sites. The "other" located teams had the highest proportion of people with severe and long-term mental health problems (66.4%), followed by those based on in-patient units (63%), those not sharing a base (63%), residentially-based teams (61%), community resource centres (59%), day centres or day hospital-based teams (57%), CMHCs (53%) and teams based in primary care (38%). These differences did not achieve statistical significance.

Table 5 – Team Base Location

Team base location	N	%
Community mental health centre	134	44.4
In-patient unit or hospital site	43	14.2
Day centre or day hospital	28	9.3
Community resource centre	25	8.3
Primary care	9	3.0
Residential	7	2.3
Other	26	8.6
Not based together	29	9.6

Table 6 shows the proportion of teams containing each discipline by team base location. Consultants and non-consultant doctors were most often

Table 6 – Percentage of Teams Containing Each Discipline by Team Base location

Discipline	CMHC	Community resource centre	Day centre/ hospital	In-patient or hospital site	Residential	Primary care	Other	Not based together
CPNs	94.8	96.0	78.6	95.3	85.7	88.9	96.2	96.6
Social workers	90.3	84.0	75.0	79.1	85.7	77.8	88.5	89.7
Administrative staff	93.3	84.0	85.7	79.1	14.0	88.9	88.5	51.7
Nurses other than CPNs	60.3	24.0	53.6	16.3	14.3	11.1	23.1	41.4
Occupational therapists	70.1	56.0	78.6	76.7	42.9	66.7	42.3	69.0
Generic/support workers	41.0	36.0	35.7	34.9	42.9	35.3	53.8	13.8
Consultant psychiatrists	82.1	76.0	89.3	67.4	42.9	55.6	76.9	96.6
Other doctors	66.2	52.0	75.0	65.1	42.9	66.7	69.2	86.2
Clinical psychologists	79.9	64.0	71.4	58.1	57.1	66.7	69.2	65.5
Others	35.1	24.0	25.0	18.6	71.4	11.1	26.9	10.3
Other specialist therapists	37.3	16.0	42.9	44.2	14.3	22.2	15.4	13.8
Volunteer staff	28.4	12.0	10.7	2.3	14.3	0	3.8	6.9

Table 7 – Service User and Community Member Involvement

Level of involvement	Yes, occurs now		No, but planned in next three months		No, and not planned	
	N	%	N	%	N	%
Regular surveys or collection of information on user views (beyond individual case work)	129	42.7	97	32.1	72	23.6
Routine user attendance at service management/steering group or business meeting with users having an *advisory* role	69	22.8	52	17.2	175	57.9
Routine user attendance at service management/steering group or business meeting with users having a *decision-making* role	25	8.3	50	16.6	218	72.2
Routine community member attendance in service management/steering group or business meeting with members having an *advisory* role	75	24.8	25	8.3	188	62.3
Routine community member attendance in service management/steering group or business meeting with members having a *decision-making* role	52	17.2	23	7.6	208	68.9

found in teams that were not based together. CPNs were the most ubiquitous discipline although found least often in day centres or day hospitals. Non-CPN nurses were concentrated in CMHCs, day hospitals or day centres, and in teams not based together. Occupational therapists and other specialist therapists were most often found in day centres or day hospitals and in teams on hospital sites.

Primary care-based teams were significantly smaller than both CMHC-based and Day centre or day hospital-based teams. Team base was also significantly associated with the number of people joining the CMHT in the last year with significantly more people joining both residential and "other" teams when compared with teams based in community resource centres.

Service user and community member involvement

Table 7 shows the three levels of user involvement and two level of community member involvement investigated. For each question respondents were asked to indicate whether the activity occurs now, does not occur but is planned within the next quarter, or is not planned at all.

Overall, the greater the powers of users and community members the less frequently involvement occurred now and the less it was planned to occur. It is of some concern that 72.2% of CMHTs not only did not involve service users in decision-making in management but also had no plans to do so. Teams were prepared to offer more responsibility to community members in general, although here too the proportions are small. Nonetheless this minimal involvement does represent an improvement from the 1987–8 survey when only 12% of CMHCs had any user involvement in management and only 16% conducted user surveys.

Team management – The sharing of leadership

In the 1987–8 survey less than 10% of CMHCs had a manager with overall responsibility for team functioning. In contrast, 74.5% of teams in the present survey reported that the team had a "team manager or coordinator". Despite this, on the question "to what extent is responsibility for team leadership or management tasks shared in the team" only 30.4% of teams reported that "one person is responsible for all leadership and management tasks". A similar number of teams reported that "tasks [were] shared among all team members but not equally" (30.8%). It is not

Table 8 – Sharing of Leadership or Management Tasks by Whether Teams had a Team Coordinator or Manager (% of Total)

Extent of shared leadership or management in the team

Team coordinator or manager?	One person		Two people		More than two – not the whole team		All team members – not equally		All team members – equally		Total	
	N	%	N	%	N	%	N	%	N	%	N	%
Yes	80	36.0	34	15.3	40	18.0	54	24.3	14	6.3	222	74.2
No	11	14.3	2	2.6	15	19.5	38	49.4	11	14.3	77	25.8
Total	91	30.4	36	12.0	55	18.4	92	30.8	25	8.4	299	100.0

known whether this indicates attempts at "democratic" team structures or simply a management vacuum. Only 8.4% of teams reported that leadership or management tasks were shared "equally among all team members". As would be predicted the existence of a team manager or coordinator was associated with the sharing of team leadership roles (see Table 8) with greater likelihood of responsibility being located in one or two people. The absence of a coordinator or manager was also associated with team members sharing responsibility.

Team management – Who manages what?

Respondents were asked to indicate who had most responsibility for the 12 responsibilities shown in Table 9. The overall percentages reveal that team managers or coordinators had most tasks assigned to them overall, followed by the "Team as a whole". Individual managers or planners outside the team and management or steering groups played a very minor role except in deciding the client group of the team and assessing the mental health needs of the local community. Even on these items the "Team as a whole" had ultimate responsibility most frequently. Only 38.4% of teams used the "Management or steering group" response on any item.

The fact that the team as a whole was most frequently ultimately responsible for assessing the mental health needs of the local community and defining the client group of the team suggests an absence of strategic management in the planning and operation of CMHTs as part of a wider network of local provision. The findings also suggest that despite the prevalence of team managers or coordinators a management vacuum pervades *within* teams. The allocation of cases to team practitioners was regarded by Ovretveit (1993) as the defining responsibility of team managers. For 51% of teams this was undertaken by the "Team as a whole" and only 20% by team coordinators or managers. The "Team as a whole" also dominated when deciding which referrals the team accepted day-to-day. These findings suggest that, despite the fact that around three-quarters of CMHTs had team managers or coordinators, ultimate responsibility for team management tasks remained dispersed within the team or undefined with little involvement of outside managers.

Where teams had team managers or coordinators they most frequently had ultimate responsibility for managing the team day-to-day, liaising

Table 9 – Percentage Allocation of Most Responsibility for Management Tasks

Management responsibility	Team manager or coordinator	Team's senior doctor. e.g. consultant or senior registrar	Individual team members	Professional line managers	Other individual managers or planners outside team	Management or steering group	Team as a whole	No one takes most charge
Deciding the client group of the team	6.1	3.4	7.1	4.0	10.4	22.6	42.8	3.7
Deciding which referrals the team accepts day-to-day	12.2	3.1	20.7	2.7	0	0.3	58.6	2.4
Deciding when team members should close cases	6.4	1.4	68.1	3.7	0	0.7	17.6	2.0
Allocating cases to team members	19.8	2.0	18.4	2.0	0	1.0	51.2	5.5
Clinical supervision of team members	14.8	3.8	14.5	50.0	2.1	0	10.7	4.1
Authorising team members' leave	32.9	0	4.4	55.4	1.7	0.3	3.7	1.7
Liaising with senior management over team issues	55.0	8.7	4.4	16.4	0	5.4	9.4	0.7
Representing the team at public meetings	38.2	4.4	18.9	9.1	1.7	4.1	14.2	9.5
Over-ruling the clinical decisions of team members if necessary	20.3	21.3	0.7	32.5	0.7	2.8	9.1	12.6
Managing the day-to-day running of the team	62.0	2.4	6.1	6.4	0.3	1.0	13.8	8.1
Organising the evaluation and/or review of team policy and practice	42.8	3.3	1.3	6.0	1.7	13.4	29.8	1.7
Assessing the mental health service needs of the local community	13.2	2.4	2.4	1.7	21.7	19.3	28.1	11.2
Overall percentage	27.0	4.7	13.9	15.8	3.4	5.9	24.1	5.3

with senior management over team issues, organising evaluation or review, representing the team at public meetings and authorising leave. Their role was thus clearly identified with operational management rather than professional management. There is, however, a danger that where operational management is weak, the distinction between operational and professional management responsibilities becomes blurred. One respondent wrote on the questionnaire to lament the absence of a team manager/coordinator: "No team management structure exists other than professional line management. Lack of a team manager/coordinator poses difficulties for [the] team and tends to reinforce the traditional role of consultant psychiatrist as team leader".

The team's senior doctor rarely had ultimate responsibility for management tasks except in the area of "over-ruling the decisions of team members if necessary". However, even on this task professional line managers were most frequently assigned responsibility. They were also most frequently ultimately responsible for clinical supervision.

Significantly fewer people left teams where responsibility for screening referrals day to day was undertaken by a team manager or coordinator when compared with teams where the team's senior doctor or professional line managers undertook the task. Fewer people also left teams where the team manager or no one took ultimate responsibility for overruling clinical decisions compared with teams where the senior doctor was ultimately responsible. These findings offer tentative evidence for lower turnover among less medically dominated teams.

Team Process

Accessing services – Offering the first contact point in the locality

170 teams (56.7%) reported offering the "first contact point for all mental health referrals in their locality or sector". Teams offering first contact had significantly smaller proportions of people with severe and long-term mental health problems on their caseloads. Teams offering first contact had been taking referrals for significantly longer than those that did not (mean = 4.45 versus 3.26 years) and had significantly larger FTE input from consultant psychiatrists, other doctors, CPNs, clinical psychologists, administrative staff and social workers.

Accessing services – Accepted sources of referral

Respondents were asked to indicate who referrals were accepted from. Open referral networks were most frequent, although if referral was restricted it was often to exclude self-referrals (see Table 10). Self-referral was accepted by 67.6% of teams overall and 73.9% of those based in CMHCs. This compares with 79% of CMHCs in the 1987–8 survey. Of the 26 teams with some other restricted range of referrers, referral via or approved by GPs was mentioned by seven teams and limiting self-referral to people already known to the service was mention by three teams. The remainder described other unique constellations of referrers including police, probation services, education, long stay wards in psychiatric hospitals, Citizen Advice Bureaux, women's refuges, and "acute" mental health centres.

Table 10 – Sources of Accepted Referrals

	N	%
Any member of the community, health and social services staff, police, relatives, friends, and self-referrers	160	53.3
Any health and social services professional (including GPs) and self-referrers	43	14.3
Any health and social services professional but not self-referrers	67	22.3
Doctors only	4	1.3
Some other restricted range of referrers	26	8.7

Accessing services – Receipt of referral

Table 11 shows who referrals were made to in the team. Referrals via team members clearly predominate. Many teams used the "other" category to indicate the "team as a whole" and so this is indicated separately. This was clearly seen by respondents as different from referral to a "single referral point" or "any team member".

Various combinations of referral either to individual practitioners, particular professions or the team as a whole via managers dominated in the "other" category. Referral via the team leader or coordinator *or* direct to team members was mentioned by five teams. A further five emphasised the team as a whole or direct referral to individuals as the available options. One team took referrals via the team coordinator except in emergencies in which case referral to individual team members was possible. Four teams stressed that referrals were made via the team's senior medical member and then subsequently allocated. For two of these an exception was made for referral to psychologists who could take direct referrals.

Some teams described different access points for different referrers. In one team consultants could refer to any team member while referrals from others went to the team as a whole for allocation. One team allowed direct referral for particular activities (such as art therapy or anxiety management). Two teams identified duty systems, two referral to sub-groups within the team and one took referrals via a case manager.

Comments suggested that some teams were aiming to achieve more integrated referral pathways, for example through "Strongly encourag[ing] team referrals...", or "Aiming for referral to a team coordinator". One respondent made clear that referral to individual team members was seen as the default option, stating that "In the absence of a team base and coordinator, referrals are received by each discipline and then pooled".

Table 11 – Points of Access for Receipt of Referral

Point of access	N	%
Non-medical team leader/manager only	15	5.0
Team doctor only	7	2.3
Some other single referral point	41	13.6
Any team member	159	52.8
Team as a whole	32	10.6
Other	47	15.6

There was no significant association between the team's caseload composition and the source or method of receipt of referrals. In particular, no evidence of self-referral leading to increased referral of people with less severe mental health problems was found (in common with Sayce, Craig and Boardman, 1991; Marriott *et al.*, 1993).

Pooling of referrals

171 teams (56.6%) pooled all their referrals before allocation for assessment (excluding emergency referrals needing to be seen very rapidly). A further 81 (26.8%) pooled some of their referrals and 50 (16.6%) pooled none. There was no significant association between pooling and caseload composition.

Sharing an office base was associated with the pooling of referrals. Among teams sharing a base 58.6% pooled all referrals, 27.8% pooled some and 13.6% did not pool any. This compares with 37.9%, 17.2% and 44.8% respectively among the 29 teams that did not share a base. The *proportion* of the team sharing a base was also associated with the pooling of referrals with a significantly higher proportion of people sharing the base among teams who pooled all referrals when compared with those that pooled only some.

Teams that received referrals as a team or via single access points were significantly more likely to pool their referrals than teams receiving referrals via individual team members or "other" methods.

Frequency of clinical review meetings

Table 12 shows how often teams had "arranged meetings to formally discuss clinical work". The majority of teams had weekly meetings. That so few met daily may reflect the low priority given to providing a rapid response to crises. Frequency of clinical review meetings was unrelated to any other variable.

Integration of record keeping

Respondents were asked if the team used a "shared record keeping system for information collected on work with clients/patients". A single integrated system of records was reported by 114 (37.7%) teams. A further 101 (33.4%) shared some of their records (e.g. for individual service planning or assessment). In 79 (26.2%) teams each profession kept their own separate records, and eight teams used "other" arrangements. Comments supplied with the "other" response suggested that these teams were moving towards integrated record keeping or had separate systems for different staff or client groups.

Table 12 – Frequency of Clinical Review Meetings

Frequency	N	%
At least once a day	13	4.3
Between two and four times a week	77	25.5
Once a week	187	61.9
Once a fortnight	15	5.0
Once a month	4	1.3
Less than once a month	0	0
Never	1	0.3
Other	5	1.7

The extent of shared record keeping was also associated with whether a base was shared. Among teams sharing a base 40.7% shared all record keeping, 33.7% shared some, 22.7% did not share records and 2.9% used some other arrangement. For teams not sharing a base the proportions were 10.3%, 31%, 58.6% and none respectively.

Services offered

Respondents were asked to indicate whether 30 activities concerned with work with users was undertaken directly by the team. For 20 items they were also given the alternative of indicating whether the team referred on to another agency for the activity. The percentage of teams undertaking the activities is shown in Table 13.

The 1987–8 survey highlighted the small number of CMHCs undertaking activities of particular relevance to people with severe and long-term mental health problems such as support for carers (12% in their survey), occupational therapy (11%) and practical assistance (5%). Clearly many more CMHTs are now undertaking these activities although psychotherapy and counselling remain the most ubiquitous activities.

Table 13 – Percentage of Teams Offering Care-related Services

Services	% undertaking
Therapy or counselling for individuals	97.0
Multidisciplinary direct work with clients following assessment	93.9
Individual service planning	93.9
Consultation to mental health workers from other agencies	92.9
Support/education for carers	91.2
Services particularly for people with severe and long-term mental health problems	88.9
Assessment of activities of daily living (e.g. using money, personal hygiene, etc)	88.8
Promotion of self help	85.2
Multidisciplinary assessment – two or more disciplines at the same time	81.0
Formal assessments under the 1983 Mental Health Act	79.4
Training in activities of daily living	77.6
Drug treatments (other than depot clinics)	75.3
Publicising the service (i.e. more than just word of mouth)	74.0
Group therapy	73.1
Immediate response to crisis in the situation in which the crisis is happening	71.1
Practical 'hands-on' help with day-to-day problems (e.g. shopping, transport)	69.7
Therapy or counselling for families	67.6
Services particularly for people who have never used mental health services before	66.7
Physical space for outside agencies to use	58.3
Depot clinics	56.1
Public education (e.g. on preventing mental health problems)	48.4
Accommodation	48.3
Day care or other occupation	46.1
Drop in/walk-in/open-access facility	46.0
Services particularly for women	41.5
Services particularly for people whose behaviour services find "challenging" or "difficult to manage"	31.0
Work opportunities	24.1
Client access to team members after working hours and at weekends	23.0
Direct purchase of services by practitioners or case (or care) managers controlling budgets	17.0
Services particularly for people from specific ethnic groups	12.9

Teams offering access to team members after hours and at weekends, services for people whose behaviour is "challenging", services particularly for people with severe and long-term mental health problems, work opportunities, practical help with everyday problems, and assessment of activities of daily living (ADL) had a significantly larger proportion of people with severe and long-term mental health problems on their caseloads than those that did not. Teams offering services particularly for women, services particularly for people who have never used services before and formal mental health act assessments had a significantly smaller percentage of people with severe and long-term mental health problems.

The size of the team was associated with the absolute number of activities undertaken (r = 0.46). Specifically, significantly larger teams offered crisis intervention, day care or other forms of occupation, specific services for women, formal mental health act assessments, open access (e.g. though offering a drop-in service), ADL assessment, and group therapy.

Table 14 illustrates the relationships between the FTE contribution of different disciplines and activities. The plus signs in the table indicate that for that activity the FTE of the corresponding discipline is significantly greater for teams that undertake that activity than for those that do not. Clearly this cannot be taken to infer that discipline is responsible for the activity taking place since both disciplines and activities may reflect particular forms of teams. Moreover, the existence of certain disciplines may have lead the respondents to assume that the activity was taking place thereby creating spurious associations. However, the associations do form a predictable pattern with doctors being associated with drug treatments, depot clinics, crisis intervention and mental health act assessments, and occupational therapists associated with assessment and training in ADL, practical 'hands-on' help, day care or other occupation and services for women. Clinical psychologists were associated with group therapy, the promotion of open access and services for women. There was significantly less input from psychologists where teams provided services specifically for people whose behaviour was seen as "challenging".

An analysis of team-base location and services offered revealed that CMHCs and community resource centres were most likely to offer

Table 14 – Associations between input from disciplines (FTE) and services offered

Services offered	CPN	Social worker	Admin staff	Nurse other than CPN	OT	Generic/ support worker	Consultant psychiatrist	Doctors (other than consultants)	Clinical psychologist	Others	Other therapists	Volunteer staff
Therapy for individuals	+											
Multidisciplinary direct work			+									
Consultation to other agencies	+											
Support/education for carers	+											
Services for severe or long-term problems	+									+		
Assessment of ADL					++							
Formal MHA assessments	++	++	++		++		++	++				
Training in ADL					++	+						
Drug treatments							++	++				
Group therapy				+					+			
Immediate response to crisis					+	++	+	++				
Practical 'hands-on' help				+								
Therapy for families												
Services for new clientele	+											+
Physical space	+		++								+	
Depot clinics	++		++				++	++				
Public education		+										
Accommodation												
Day care or other occupation				+	++			+				
Drop in/walk-in/open-access		+	++		++	++				+		
Services for women	+	+	++		++				+	+		
Services for "challenging" behaviour									– –			
Work opportunities						++		+				
Access out of hours				+								

Key: + significantly higher FTE at p < 0.01 in teams offering the corresponding activity, ++ p < 0.001, – – significantly lower FTE at p < 0.001

physical space for other agencies to use, and along with primary care settings most often provided services for "new clientele". Primary care settings were least likely to provide specialised services for people with severe and long-term mental health problems. It is perhaps more surprising that they also provided open access least frequently.

Access after working hours and at weekends is often seen as a priority by service users (Shepherd and Murray, 1994; Morgan, 1993). This was available from only 23% of teams. These same teams had a significantly higher input from generic/support workers and non-CPN nurses when compared with teams that did not offer out of hours access. This service was most often offered by teams based in community resource centres (34.8%) and least often by primary care (12.5%) or CMHC-based (19.4%) teams.

An analysis of the extent to which activities clustered together revealed that ADL assessment, training in ADL and practical hands-on help were significantly inter-associated. Services for people with severe and long-term mental health problems were associated with practical hands-on help and day care or other occupation. Group therapy was associated with services for women and offering physical space for other agencies to use; services for women was also associated with services for "new clientele"; publicising the service was associated with public education; and the provision of work opportunities was associated with day care and other occupation, and the provision of accommodation. Crisis intervention was only associated with formal Mental Health Act assessments, suggesting that the two activities may have been synonymous. Only 57 (27.3%) of teams offering crisis intervention also offered out of hours access suggesting that a maximum of 18% of the sample offered a 24-hour, seven-days a week crisis response. These teams were most often found in CMHCs (31.6%), or in-patient units or hospitals (19.3%).

Access to hospital beds

Table 15 shows that all teams used hospital beds and most had direct access to hospital beds via a team member. Of the 11 teams using the "other" category three teams arranged admission through GPs and two teams were fully integrated with in-patient wards with shared management of both services.

Table 15 – Team Access to Hospital Beds

Method of access	N	%
Team has direct access to hospital beds via a team member (e.g. team psychiatrist)	219	72.5
Referral necessary to workers outside the team (e.g. hospital-based duty psychiatrist or casualty department)	72	23.8
Hospital beds not used	0	0
Other	11	3.6

Significantly more FTE psychiatrists and other doctors operated in teams with direct access when compared with those where referral was necessary.

An increased proportion of teams offering the first contact point for mental health services in the locality, formal assessments under the mental health act, crisis intervention and drug treatment other than depot had direct access to beds. This may be because these teams also contained more FTE consultants and other doctors providing these activities.

Responsibility for planning and providing care following admission

Table 16 shows the transfer of responsibilities following admission. The largest proportion of teams reported that although the team continued to provide care on admission, responsibility for planning care was transferred to in-patient staff. The remainder were divided between those teams where responsibility for planning care was retained but most care was provided by in-patient staff and those where responsibility for both planning and providing care was transferred to in-patient staff. Only seven teams reported retaining the major responsibility for planning and providing care during in-patient stays.

Table 16 –Transfer of Responsibilities on Admission

Transfer of responsibilities on admission	N	%
Responsibility for planning and providing care transferred to in-patient staff	82	27.2
Responsibility for planning care transferred to in-patient staff but team continues to provide care	126	41.7
Team retains responsibility for planning care but most care provided by in-patient staff	84	27.8
Team retains major responsibility for planning and providing care during in-patient stay	7	2.3

The transfer of responsibility was associated with the FTE contribution of social workers in the team with significantly more input to teams that transfer responsibility for provision only compared with teams that transfer all responsibility, and those that transfer planning only.

Case/care management

Case/care management systems were reported as operational in 155 (51.8%) teams. However, 28 (18.3%) respondents who replied "yes" to the question "Does the team operate a case/care management system" then went on to state that the team plans to implement case/care management within the next three months (ignoring the prompt to proceed directly to the next section if they had answered the previous questions on case/care management). Respondents may have been differentiating case from care management and referring to the April 1st 1993 deadline for implementation of community care when social services care managers assumed assessment and purchasing responsibilities. A conservative estimate of teams practising case/care management at the time of the survey would exclude this group putting the number of teams at 122 (40.4%). Of teams that reported that they were not operating care or case management 53.6% reported that they would be implementing it within the next three months. 22 % of the sample were not operating case/care management and had no plans to do so in the next quarter.

A keyworker system other than case or care management was reported as operational in 251 (83.1%) teams. Of these 48.4% also operated a case/care management system. Teams that provided case/care management or keyworking did not report a significantly larger proportion of people with severe and long-term mental health problems on their caseloads.

Among the teams operating case/care management, 85.7% viewed it as "one of a number of tasks of professional practitioners. Only 9.7% reported that staff responsible for case/care management [were] solely case/care managers". Of the seven teams (4.5%) using the "other" category, two referred to case/care management as a service linked to the team catering for a small number of clients with special needs. One team felt both categories applied.

Other Information Obtained in the Course of the Research

Respondents had the opportunity to volunteer comments on their own team. These were drawn from a free text item at the end of the questionnaires and in the course of the telephone survey.

The most frequent comments concerned organisational change. Many districts were still in the process of developing multidisciplinary teams. Often these developments had been preceded by organisational changes to locality or sector based services. Many teams appeared to be working towards stronger management at team level, location on a single site, single access points for the receipt of referrals and increased user involvement. The Care Programme approach seemed to have prompted multidisciplinary working in many areas but not necessarily the development of multidisciplinary teams.

The view that "to be truly called a multidisciplinary team one has to have equal commitment from all the services involved" was typical. One respondent complained that all members had commitments elsewhere and there was concern about having to "beg and borrow" professional time. Social workers, psychologists and consultant psychiatrists were most often cited as lacking adequate commitment to the team. Lack of team integration was also reflected in concern about diffuse team boundaries (e.g. with "rehab" teams).

Other reasons given for lack of development or arrested development of multidisciplinary teams included resource constraints and changes in organisation to Trust status. A number of districts were undergoing trust status applications with associated changes in finance. A particular problem raised by funding constraints was difficulties in securing staff other than CPNs. Problems filling occupational therapy and psychology posts were particularly stressed and borne out in the analysis of team composition. Another common finding was that in some areas the local authority's financial constraints had led to non-replacement of social workers.

Confusion concerning team-level management was expressed. This included ambiguity about "management" versus "coordination, and team managers not being "core" staff within the team.

The role of GPs as purchasers also gave rise to concerns. Respondents feared that GPs would tend to contract with specific disciplines for provision while remaining largely ignorant of the advantages of a team approach. GP purchasing was also seen as a threat to sectorised services and therefore to multidisciplinary teams aiming to provide services to people within a particular area. Finally, the greater purchasing role of GPs was predicted to shift demands for service provision towards those with less severe mental health problems.

Discussion

A survey method can only give broad indications of the actual structure and process of CMHTs. Since the study was cross-sectional it is not possible to make definite statements about direction of causality. Nonetheless, some important themes emerge from the findings.

The growth of fragmented CMHTs

CMHTs appear to be still in the ascendant, increasing both in number and size. However, with the exception of nurses, social workers, occupational therapists and generic/support workers, most team members offer only limited part-time input. The present study also particularly highlighted the comparatively small FTE input from consultants and other doctors, clinical psychologists, and other therapists.

Large amounts of part-time working was negatively associated with the team's dedication of caseload to people with severe and long-term mental health problems. Avoiding fragmented teams may be important in promoting adequate and reliable access to an appropriate range of skills, and the intensive and continuous community support required for work with complex on-going difficulties. Clear team boundaries may also be important to the development of a strong team identity and peer support

A shift towards work with people with severe and long-term mental health problems?

Around a third of the CMHTs studied had two-thirds or more of their caseloads dedicated to people with severe and long-term mental health problems. Although comparative data is unavailable, this may represent a shift towards affording greater priority to work with people with severe and long-term mental health problems among an increasing proportion of CMHTs.

The finding that urban teams had a higher proportion of people with severe and long-term mental health problems would be predicted from previous literature on "social drift" of disadvantaged groups to urban environments (Warner, 1985). Although there was greater turnover among urban staff it is notable that there was no association between team caseload composition and the numbers of staff leaving or joining CMHTs.

A trend towards the provision of more relevant services

Patmore and Weaver (1991) observed that provision of services of specific relevance militated against the usual neglect of people with severe and long-term mental health problems. One of their more successful teams had a day centre, the catchment depot clinic, outpatient psychiatry, a service that would visit severely distressed people at home, and groups for families and carers.

Overall, the availability of relevant services seems to have improved since the 1987–8 survey. Certain services offered were associated with a higher proportion of people with severe and long-term mental health problems on the team's caseload, notably psycho-social interventions such as access out of working hours and at weekends, work opportunities, practical help with everyday problems, and assistance in developing activities of daily living. However, the availability of round-the-clock crisis intervention and services particularly for people from minority ethnic groups remains particularly limited.

Many ostensibly relevant activities were not associated with higher proportions of people with severe and long-term mental health problems. For example, formal Mental Health Act assessments, crisis intervention, drug treatments (including depot clinics), training in ADL, support or education for carers, keyworking and case/care management. The finding that formal assessments were associated with a smaller proportion of people with severe and long-term mental health problems was particularly anomalous. That it was also associated with the 56.7% of CMHTs offering the first contact point for all mental health referrals in their localities may reflect an emphasis on assessment at the expense of including people with severe and long-term mental health problems in on-going caseloads.

Some features of integrated team operation clustered together. Pooling of referrals was associated with the availability of a team base, a high proportion of the team sharing the base, and the receipt of referrals via single access points. Nonetheless these features were not associated with increased dedication of caseload to people with severe and long-term mental health problems.

The need for open but targeted access

Offering a "comprehensive" service to all mental health service users is a cornerstone of CMHC ideology (e.g. Morris and Davidson, 1992). This usually means attempting to offer a wide range of services to a wide range of people and overall CMHCs have been credited with increasing accessibility to an increased volume and range of community-based services (Dowell and Ciarlo, 1983; Sayce, Craig and Boardman, 1991). However, this very accessibility has also been cited as one of the reasons why teams have tended to become congested with referrals of people who do not have severe and long-term mental health problems.

Providing a single access point for all mental health referrals in a locality is often seen as one method for making services accessible to a wide range of people. The present study found that CMHTs that provided this service had significantly smaller proportions of people with severe and long-term mental health problems on their caseloads. It is also notable, however, that open referral policies were not associated with a significantly larger proportion of people with less severe problems. This suggests that in order to maintain a focus on people with the most severe mental health problems, services need to accept referrals from a wide range of sources but then "gate-keep" to ensure that only the team's defined client group are taken on for assessment and on-going work.

Locating the team – Time to abandon the CMHC?

Primary care-based teams had the smallest proportion of people with severe and long-term mental health problems on their caseloads. A recent study of a primary care based team found a marked increase in rates of inception to care particularly for less severe mental health problems (Jackson *et al.*, 1993). They report "conflict for staff between the demands of anxious and unhappy people with overwhelming social and domestic difficulties on the one hand, and the formally ill but often less demanding patients on the other" (p.377, *ibid*). Morris and Davidson (1992) have argued that CMHCs should remain located in primary care in order to incorporate the GP interest in the strategic planning of mental health services. However, it is unclear how this will help to manage the tension between GP demands and the needs of a more severely distressed, socially deprived and less vocal minority. A more rational approach may be the "Integrated primary care model" (Strathdee and Thornicroft, 1992) whereby members of both acute or crisis intervention and continuing-care elements of sector teams liaise with general practice (and other agencies) and provide assessments and subsequent interventions in primary care settings when appropriate.

In the earlier Sainsbury Centre survey, only 81 CMHCs could be identified in the UK (despite a 95% response rate). The present study suggests an approximate three-fold increase in their number by 1993 and shows that they remain the main base for CMHTs. However, aside from primary care-based teams, CMHCs had the lowest proportions of people with severe and long-term mental health problems. The "comprehensive" CMHC-based approach to team working where a wide variety of services are provided on site to all comers may not be appropriate when aiming to meet the needs of people with severe and long-term mental health problems. That the "other" located (mainly office-based) teams had the highest proportion may argue instead for a team-base where service users are not seen for clinical work and help is provided in ordinary environments such as the person's home (e.g. Burns *et al.*, 1993, Merson *et al.*, 1992; Muijen *et al.*, 1992) and primary care settings as described above.

The need for stronger external and internal team management

CMHT provision needs to have a considered role determined by locality-based needs assessment and the availability and operation of other local provision (Strathdee and Thornicroft, 1992). Shaping this role cannot be left entirely to practitioners who may be unable or unwilling to take this wider view. Patmore and Weaver (1991) ascribe the failure of CMHTs to prioritise people with severe and long-term mental health problems to an abdication by senior management of their responsibilities for determining the policy and the practice of CMHTs. This failure of strategic management is also suggested by the present findings with outside managers and planners, and management or steering groups only occasionally having the final say on important strategic matters.

While there does appear to be a significant shift towards formal teams with managers or coordinators, the team as a whole continues to carry a major burden of responsibility. It cannot be determined from the present study whether this indicates attempts at democratic team structures or a management vacuum. The lack of evidence for strong external management to shape internal management roles would suggest the latter.

User participation – Poor but getting better

User and community member participation in management, although more prevalent than in 1987–8, remains insufficient. A large proportion of teams appear to have failed to appreciate the imperative to create opportunities for genuine participation, although paradoxically it seems that community members in general are provided with more opportunities for participation that service users themselves. While this may partly reflect negative attitudes towards the merits of user participation and the capabilities of service users in management, it seems likely that the need for training and adequate resources to create the optimal conditions for effective participation will also be important.

The role of medical staff

The comparatively small FTE input from consultant psychiatrists may contribute to neglect of people with severe and long-term mental health problems among a large proportion of CMHTs. Patmore and Weaver (1991) observed that where GPs had to chose to refer to a consultant or a CMHT, 80% of direct referrals to the CMHT were "new clientele" without significant histories of psychiatric care or psychotic diagnoses. In order to avoid this, consultants need to be more strongly identified with CMHTs.

Control of admissions has been shown to be critical to services aiming to reduce the use of in-patient beds (Stein and Test, 1980; Hoult, 1986; Dean and Gadd, 1990). The high proportion of teams with direct access to beds is a promising development and underlines the importance of medical input to teams in achieving direct access to hospital beds when required.

One reason for the comparatively small input from psychiatrists into CMHTs may be the limited management responsibilities allocated to them there. Isaacs and Bebbington (1991) advocated that psychiatrists perform a range of management tasks such as taking responsibility for establishing case registers, ensuring the quality of documentation, overseeing referrals to the team and representing the team before senior management and at meetings concerned with service development. It is unclear what qualifies psychiatrists to undertake these tasks. Muijen (1993) also described a range of management roles for consultant psychiatrists in community care but stressed the need for a greater recognition among psychiatrists of the need for high levels of individual responsibility among other team members, the rejection of rigid hierarchies, increased emphasis on psycho-social models of care, and clarity concerning the diversity of different forms of responsibility to be assigned (e.g. care coordinating and operational). It is clear that the role of psychiatrists in CMHTs will be invaluable in future but may be more clearly and narrowly defined than previously.

The numbers of people joining and leaving teams must be interpreted cautiously as there are many reasons why practitioners may join or leave teams aside from the attractions or otherwise of the CMHT itself (e.g. Knapp *et al.*, 1992). However, the familiar dissent within teams over the assumption of inappropriate leadership roles by consultant psychiatrists may partially explain the higher numbers of people leaving teams where the team's senior doctor has most responsibility for screening referrals and over-ruling clinical decisions when necessary.

The role of social workers and care management

The small number of teams retaining responsibility for planning and providing care on admission is a source of concern and highlights the need for more flexible arrangements. The present study highlights the social worker's important role in ensuring continuity in planning at this critical point. There is a risk that this will be undermined if their new care management roles take them away from the day-to-day work of CMHTs (Mental Health Act Commission, 1993; Morris and Davidson, 1992). The high prevalence of joint agency funding and management in the present survey is a hopeful sign.

It is also encouraging that the majority of CMHTs integrated case or care management within the existing roles of professional practitioners. This is very much in line with recommendations for integrated joint working at team level in order to promote "seamless" services and effective user engagement (Onyett, 1992; Ford, Cooke, and Repper, 1992).

Looking to the Future: Recommendations and Conclusions

When seen in the context of other recent research some tentative recommendations can be drawn from the present study.

1. A "comprehensive" CMHC-model may not be a good approach to serving people with severe and long-term mental health problems. While it is appropriate to remain maximally accessible through an open referral policy, more attention should be paid to establishing CMHTs with explicit client eligibility criteria and mechanisms for gate-keeping referrals.

2. CMHT's allocation of resources to people with severe and long-term mental health problems is likely to be maintained through the provision of relevant services such as out of hours and weekend access, work opportunities, practical assistance with everyday problems and work on activities of daily living.

3. Larger teams may be required to achieve this.

4. It may be that such services are not best provided at the team's base. Peripatetic teams that adopt more assertive models of service delivery merit further development and evaluation.

5. For administrative purposes however, a team base shared by a large proportion of the team may be crucial to the development of integrated access points, multidisciplinary pooling of referrals for allocation and integrated record keeping.

6. Avoiding fragmented teams with many part-time posts may promote the continuity of contact required for work with people with severe and long-term mental health problems. Greater full-time involvement from particular disciplines such as psychiatry, psychology and occupational therapy may also be critical. Whether the current paucity of input reflects lack of resources or ambivalence on the part of the disciplines themselves remains to be seen. However, greater investment in training to meet the challenges of community-based work will be invaluable in attracting staff and making the best use of the human resources available.

7. All these recommendations require stronger operational management at team level rather than reliance on the team as a whole to make important strategic and operational decisions. This in turn requires improved strategic joint planning and "ring-fencing" of resources for services for people with severe and long-term mental health problems.

It was apparent that this is a period of great upheaval for many teams. The need to integrate social services-led care management and health-led care programming while dealing with the effects of GP fund-holding and, in some cases, inadequate reprovision following hospital closure may yet provide a fatal challenge to CMHTs in their present form. Their best hopes lie in effective and equitable joint health, social services and GP purchasing strategies. Increased joint funding and an integrated approach to care management are two hopeful signs from the present study. Through effective joint working from the highest levels down we can become more confident of the future for coherent and coordinated team working for people with severe and long-term mental health problems.

References

Anciano, D. and Kirkpatrick, A. (1990) CMHTs and clinical psychology: the death of a profession? *Clinical Psychology Forum*, 26, 9 – 12.

Bachrach, L. L. (1980) Overview: model programs for chronic mental patients. *American Journal of Psychiatry*, 137(9), 1023 – 1031.

Burns, T., Beadsmoore, A., Bhat, A. V., Oliver, A. and Mathers, C. (1993) A controlled trial of home-based acute psychiatric services I: Clinical and social outcome. *British Journal of Psychiatry*, 163, 49 – 54.

Dean, C. and Gadd, E. M. (1990) Home treatment for acute psychiatric illness. *British Medical Journal*, 301, 1021 – 1023.

Department of Health (1990) *Community Care in the Next Decade and Beyond*. London: HMSO.

Department of Health/Social Services Inspectorate. (1991) *Care Management and Assessment: Managers Guide*. London: HMSO.

Ford, R., Cooke, A., and Repper, J. (1992) Making a point of contact. *Nursing Times*, 88(45), 40 – 42.

Hoult, J. (1986) Community care of the acutely mentally ill. *British Journal of Psychiatry*, 149, 137 – 144

Isaacs, A. D. and Bebbington, P. E. (1991) Strategies for the management of severe psychiatric illness in the community. *International Review of Psychiatry*, 3, 71 – 82.

Jabitsky, I. M. (1988) Psychiatric teams and the psychiatrist's authority in the New York State mental health system. *New York State Journal of Medicine*, 88(11), 577 – 581.

Jackson, G., Gater, R., Goldberg, D., Tantam, D., Loftus, L. and Taylor, H. (1993) A new community mental health team based in primary care. *British Journal of Psychiatry*, 162, 375 – 384.

Knapp, M., Cambridge, P., Thomason, C., Allen, C., Beecham, J. and Darton, R. (1992) *Care in the Community: Challenge and Demonstration*. Aldershot: Gower.

Marriott, S. Malone, S., Onyett, S. and Tyrer, P. (1993) The consequences of an open referral system to a community mental health service. *Acta Psychiatrica Scandinavica*, 88, 93 – 97.

McAusland, T. (1985) *Planning and Monitoring Community Mental Health Centres.* London: Kings Fund Centre.

Mental Health Act Commission. (1993) *Fifth Biennial Report 1991 – 1993.* London. HMSO.

Merson, S., Tyrer, P., Onyett, S., Lack, S., Birkett, P., Lynch, S. and Johnson, T. (1992) Early intervention in psychiatric emergencies: a controlled clinical trial. *The Lancet*, 339, 1311 – 1314.

Morgan, S. (1993) *Community Mental Health: Practical Approaches to Long-term Problems.* London: Chapman and Hall.

Morris. D. and Davidson, L. (1992) Community mental health centres in a changing environment. *Journal of Mental Health*, 1, 295 – 299.

Muijen, M. (1993) The consultant psychiatrist and community care. *Psychiatric Bulletin*, 17, 513 – 516.

Muijen, M., Marks, I. M. Connolly, J., Ausini, B., McNamee, G. (1992) The daily living programme: Preliminary comparison of community versus hospital based treatment for the seriously mentally ill facing emergency admission. *British Journal of Psychiatry*, 160, 379 – 384.

Onyett, S. (1992) *Case Management in Mental Health.* London: Chapman and Hall.

Ovretveit, J. (1986) *Organising Multidisciplinary Community Teams.* BIOSS Working paper. Uxbridge: Brunel University.

Ovretveit, J. (1993) *Coordinating Community Care: Multidisciplinary Teams and Care Management.* Buckingham: Open University Press.

Patmore, C. and Weaver, T. (1992) Improving community services for serious mental disorders. *Journal of Mental Health*, 1, 107 – 115.

Patmore, C. and Weaver, T. (1991) *Community Mental Health Teams: Lessons for Planners and Managers.* London: Good Practices in Mental Health.

Perlman, B., Hartman, E. A. and Bosak, J. (1984) A study of mental health administrators and systems utilising a four-part urban/rural taxonomy. *Community Mental Health Journal*, 20(3), 202 – 211.

Sayce, L., Craig, T. K. J. and Boardman, A. P. (1991) The development of community mental health centres in the UK. *Social Psychiatry and Psychiatric Epidemiology*, 26: 14 – 20.

Shea, G. P. and Guzzo, R. A. (1987) Groups as human resources. *Research in Personnel and Human Resources Management*, 5, 323 – 356.

Shepherd, G. (1994) *The Essential Background to the Care Programme Approach – Multidisciplinary Team Working*. Paper presented at Training of Key Workers for the Care Programme Approach Conference. London. March 1994.

Shepherd, G. Murray, A. and Muijen, M. (1994) *What Kinds of Help Do People with Schizophrenia Need to Live Sucessfully in the Community? The Differing Views of Users, Family Carers and Professionals*. The Sainsbury Centre for Mental Health, London.

Stein, L. I. and Test, M. A. (1980) Alternative to mental hospital treatment I. *Archives of General Psychiatry*, 37, 392 – 397.

Strathdee, G. and Thornicroft, G. (1992) Community sectors for needs-led mental health services. In . Thornicroft, G., Brewin, C. and Wing, J. (Eds) *Measuring Mental Health Needs*. London: Royal College of Psychiatrists.

Warner, R. (1985) *Recovery from Schizophrenia*. Boston: Routledge and Kegan Paul.

Appendix

A note on statistical analysis

The paucity of existing research to guide the formulation of hypotheses for the national survey required an exploratory approach to the present study. However, since this required a great many comparisons, the risk of false positive results became highly inflated. In order to reduce this risk, only results significant at the one percent level are reported (except for *post hoc* multiple comparisons which use the five percent level of significance when examining main effects).

The chisquare coefficient was used to examine associations between nominal level variables. For two by two level crosstabulations the reported chisquare coefficient was corrected for continuity. Interval level variables were not normally distributed and so non-parametric tests were used. The Kruskal-Wallis test was used for examining associations between interval level variables and nominal level variables with more than two levels. The Mann Whitney U test was used for examining association between interval level variables and dichotomous variables. It was also used for *post hoc* multiple comparisons using significance levels modified to take account of the number of comparisons. Spearman rank correlation coefficient was used to examine relationships between interval variables.

Further details on statistical analysis can be obtained from the authors.

DEPARTMENT OF APPLIED
SOCIAL STUDIES AND
SOCIAL RESEARCH
BARNETT HOUSE
WELLINGTON SQUARE
OXFORD OX1 2ER